Rub Duck

by **J. C. Cunningham**

illustrations by **Jackie Snider**

Harcourt Brace & Company

Orlando Atlanta Austin Boston San Francisco Chicago Dallas New York Toronto London

Rub-a-dub-dub.

Duck plays in the tub.

Now it's time to run
in the sun.

But look!

Duck fell. THUD!

Duck fell down
in the mud.

Duck plays in the mud.

Duck plays in the muck.

6

But Mother Duck sees.

Rub-a-dub-duck is back

in the tub!